I0465153

Everything

&

Nothing

A collection of poems by Mr. West

Message from the author:

I want to take the time to say thank you for purchasing and reading my very first book, *Everything and Nothing*. I am a believer that a true artist lives life, feels it all and then creates after. *Everything and Nothing* is a direct reflection of myself and my life. Often times I find myself presented with a number of options only to become stuck with not being able to make a decision. I call this everything and nothing. I want all the options, but because I can't make a decision, I do not want anything at the same time...Thus, *Everything and Nothing*. This is the culmination of 5 years of growth, observation and introspection. Growing pains are real, but everything in life can be a teaching moment if you are open to it. I encourage you to read and interpret my writing for yourself and share this book with as many people as you can. Life can be difficult and my hope is that someone will read and relate to the things I've experienced and have felt. Again, thank you for purchasing and reading my debut book...*Everything and Nothing*.

I appreciate your time,

-Mr. West

The unconditional

Loving yourself
Doesn't mean you are happy all the time
It's just seeing your true self
And having that be fine

-Mr.West

Production cost

We are products of our environment
If you do not like the product your environment has made you
Change your environment

      -Mr.West

The Feeling

Sighs
...okay...
I'm ready for the world now

-Mr.West

The city fog

Moved to city that can keep up with my mind
Only to find

That I'm more at home than at home

Life is like a book
Inside there lies chapters
At some point one life stops
And another is born after
In the details are the truest of souls
Through details
The truest stories are told
Secrets as valuable as gold
Betrayals ice cold
Don't get caught looking backwards
Not comprehending
And rereading the same chapter
My hope is growth
Learning something you didn't know
Plant seeds
New seeds to sow
Roses really grow from concrete
My petals are gaining altitude
With some help of a glass or two
Is that...
Please pass that too
No clear nights living in the city
When I'm foggy it's more pretty

-Mr. West

The spot

Windy city of the west
Where I love it best
Where the foundation settled
And my feet never rest
I look to Ina's playground for peace
Top of the city to see what futures are within reach
If I never accomplish a thing
Will I be okay
Will the voice in my head finally go away
How can I live
Giving you my all
If the only that ever catches me is the fall
Don't ever do what they do
Because they are not you
And doing you is what makes them
Want to be you
Make your way
Love your way
When the marathon is over
Nobody will have anything to say

-Mr. West

Revisiting a vision

Cotton candy skies
Bring tears to my eyes
Cities beauty unmeasured
For months I watched a life die
And for months I search to find the things
To make myself whole again
I watched the pieces shatter
Day after day laid in bed
Broken
Wondering if I'd rather be dead
This is the experience I had
Grabbed what I could from this empty apartment
And hit the road
But the pieces left behind leave holes
Scattered around the city are the pieces
To bring me back to life
Healing wounds should never be scratched
But in the pain is where the inspiration is at
Cotton candy skies I sure do miss them
Clouds are clearing
Time to revisit visions

-Mr.West

30

What a decade it has been
Early years spent in the city of sin
Wasted again
Nights turned to early mornings
Mornings that we never saw
Wake up at 12 it's back to the bar
Brake to 24 and life was a chore
What a bore
Didn't really want to be here no more
Found solace in isolation
Challenged my own foundations
Moved to a city at 27 and found a home
Only to have it crumble
Rebuilt a foundation a few months ago
It's coming together I think you should know
What will stay will stay
What will go will go
No need to push no more
Just let life flow
Back on my feet and what do you know
Found a seed and a small plant began to grow
29 taught me more in a year
Than all of my twenties combined
I'm thankful for every minute of that time
What a decade it has been
...30

    -Mr.West

Selfish and Temporary

Don't post about life
I'm living it
Don't post about good deeds
I'm just giving it
Don't post about revelations or epiphanies
I've already had them
Rollin' my eyes at you
I'm looking passed them
Always on another level
Evolution don't settle
Read practice and preach
Momentary vibes are weak

    -Mr.West

The magazine

Altered state
Where it is great
Don't worry
I can handle more than you
True
I have issues
But we all do
My magazine
Is just on
Another shelf

-Mr.West

The wheel

Society is pressure
Why must I stress
Why must I measure
Let me regress if I choose
Let me lose if I choose
At least I did it may way
With my life I demand a say
Misunderstood
I would reset if I could
Relive life experience if I could
I pushed the wheel downhill at a certain age
And since
Spent most of my time trying to slow it down
But time doesn't care
As one foot digs my grave
Pressured into society game
Finding balance I stay
I'm just begging for my anxiety to go away

-Mr.West

The one who lives alone

My life is within
External pressures will never measure anything
We are just distracting from what lies within
Allow life to flow as nature intends
No need to always try and upend
The more I push back at life
The less I know
Every second is a chance to grow
Inside
External growth means nothing
Time is nothing
Everything is nothing
Except what lies within
I will never push life
I will be free from all stress
All worry
And allow life to come to me as it may
Feel everything and shed a layer of skin
And at the end of it all I will smile
For the beauty will remain within

-Mr.West

Substance(s)

If I'm ever out of food
Know I'll still have weed
Neglected nourishment
So my brain I feed
I don't ask for much these days
Little love
Little smoke
Little drink
Little conversation to make me think
Why do we act like we got it figured out
Opinions are like assholes
All shit and no substance
I need the substance
I love it
Too much and my body
I'll be above it
Just enjoy this shit
Jet life will never leave you low
So high up I'm waving at this world below

-Mr.West

Hollow man

Impatient with the most patient me
Finding it hard to embrace me
Feel like I'm on a roller coaster
Feeling sick...Hope it's almost over
It's funny how life syncs with itself
Having connections made
Like the words of a book challenging me
Telling me to live one way
But
Living is never as easy as they say
Embrace what has happen
Flow with change
I'm flowing
But the course is not without bumps
Raft just popped
Ready to jump

-Mr.West

The next move is to move

Going against the grain
Tried to replace blood with ice in my veins
It never works out to well
Outburst of emotion
Colder than my days in the Mission
Nothing left in the fridge
Just ice
Bathtub spilling over
From those unconscious nights
The wildest kind of roller coaster
Stress loaded on my shoulders
Realize my eyes encase emotion
I try hard to close them
But I always show them

I don't know how I'm moving
Or what part of me these pills are ruling
But I manage to keep moving
I just keeping moving
I keep moving
Keep moving
...Just keep moving

-Mr.West

The empty feeling

I feel defeated today
Depleted today
Searching for a reason today
To end the season some way

Deep breath in
And out

Okay

Let's figure this shit out
One of those days
When you want to break everything
And can't fake anything
If someone happens to crawl under your skin
You'll uncage the fury within
I'm just sad today
And that's okay

Deep breath in...
And out

...That helped for a second...

       -Mr. West

The revelation

It's a god
Eat
God world

-Mr.West

Polk St.

Truth is
We love being a threat
We love being what you dread
We love those thoughts you have in the back of your head
As I walk by blaring hip hop
You clutch your bag when we near
It IS us you should fear
When we think of you
Know our thoughts are clear
These thoughts you don't have to deal with
Self-hatred's real we feel it
Same blood we spill it
Same skin but different cloth
The sun made me a different shade
But instead of love
We decide to spread hate
Even though we have the same fate
We are not who you should be hating
Look up at who doing all the taking
Our lives have been compromised
Good morning it's time to rise

      -Mr.West

The loudmouth

Not good enough
For a seat at your table
So we stand while being
Serenaded by your American fable
My fingers clamp the table
And flip it in rage
You've had us in chains
Destiny rearranged
Nothing explained
Slaves we became
Hundreds and hundreds
Of years we were
Born into thought
No more valuable than dirt is
At least that's what's the word is
Strong race
Strong culture
Rid of it all
Ate my soul
Vulture
Can't stand to be my equal
Even at red lights
When my windows blare
Hip hop snares
And heavy bass vibrations
If I played sports for a living
You would be all for my congratulations

-Mr.West

The Tenderloin

There is a rage in us
Silverback rattling a cage in us
If only you could see the world the way we see it
Hear it the way we hear it
How we feel it
Created it
And how we are treated
Cannot switch shoes
But imagine if we did
Imagine if we changed lives as little kids
Understanding the world as we do and did
Concrete jungle
30 years to solidify
You lazy fucks
Give me mine

-Mr.West

The realignment

Political alignment
Is humanitarian blindness
How do we right this
Self-absorbed mindlessness
Maybe we should start
With kindness

   -Mr.West

Again?

I'm tired of waking up with a memory

-Mr.West

Two Face

Broken and erased
I would spray myself with mace
If it meant I would never have to see your face again

Growth and evolution

Then again maybe I should be thankful
For everything is a gift
The emptiest of spaces
Only leave room to find yourself
...Again

    -Mr.West

The somebody's nobodies and warmbodies

Learn to need nobody
Because a warm body ain't somebody
And somebody
Can become nobody just as fast
As they became somebody

     -Mr.West

Mission and 19th

Nights on replay
Allow me to relay
My 49 daze
Thinking of 45 ways to take the same way home
But that ain't home no more
That don't mean it don't' hurt no more
That don't mean that I don't work no more
Heart of a lion
I'll die trying to find love
Love is blind and so am I
Another sucker getting two-timed

      -Mr.West

The Mirror

I blame myself
For always giving too much of me
Living in agony
In plain sight of your ecstasy
Look at the mess we have left
And by we
I mean me
I make a mess of my emotions
I can't control my hurt
I can't stand me sometimes
I can't seem to reign them in
I can't seem to not feel
I can't seem to catch my breath
Got me thinking about him
Got me constantly in a dream state
The city is plentiful
What you fiending for today
The city will take care of ya
What you fiending for today
The thing they don't tell you about
That light at the end of the tunnel
That one there
It's just the sun
The light disappears at night
Hope is lost and I sink deeper
Accepting a blind fate
Disappointed in the morning when I wake

-Mr.West

A sons heart

I will take you for granted
And not know about all the hours
You worked for things I was handed
I will make mistakes and take too long
To learn the lessons you tried to teach
But your love was always within arm's reach
I will always think of you and if I made you proud
I'll remember the times we laughed
And talks to late in life we had aloud
I will make you mad and sometimes sad
But the older I get
The more memories I wish we had
With peers becoming parents
I see responsibility
Inherited
And understand the love they share
And how much you did
And how much you care
About the future of your kids
Weight of the world
You carried a ton
The mother lottery
I have won
Thank you for the continued love
Love
Your son

    -Mr.West

3721

I've never wanted to be sick
Until it was your heart
That mine has picked
I want to fall terribly ill and have you care for me
I want your warmth
It lets me know you are there for me
Hot soup, fresh sheets, and a box of Kleenex
Bottle of Benadryl
A nap with you would be next
Just to spend a day sick and in your arms
Knowing my heart is safe from harm
At that moment
The moment I love so deep
My heart is flooded with joy
And I feel loved

      -Mr.West

17th and church

Your body is a never-ending story that I cannot put down
I want to read your pages and bookmark your spot
Proofread, revise, I know I missed a lot
Your body is admirable
But our bodies will not last
Your mind is what I love most
I want to be your inspiration
And fuel your fire
Then admire what I desired and with that
I will become inspired to rewire and reconnect
The connection that I have become disconnected from
You will find the good in me
For there are times when I cannot see the good in myself
In you I find wealth
Not wealth as in money
Rather what honey means to a bee
You give me purpose
Because what you mean to me
Is more than I can ever express with this thing in my chest
So I will make it my life's work to make sure
That you know
What you mean to me
What I mean to you
...I love you

Mr.West

The shining

Winding down now
Pick up the pen now
Recluse
Got the juice
My vision
Time to see it through
Not for you but me
Taking lessons from Bukowski
Expose the world through
What it is I see
Give pages
Of vulnerable me
Exploit me
No Holds barred
Deepest thoughts me
Suicide me
Full of pride me
The explosive fire in me
Fear of releasing me
Scared of judgment me
How you created me
Self-hating me
Inspired me and heavily wired me
Ambitious me and frivolous me
Despite what I see
I know there's good in me
Good I need to see

-Mr.West

Trapped in my eyes

Stay strong young one
Not everything is meant for sun
Not every battle is meant to be won...or lost for that matter
I find peace in believing that life has no purpose
We are meant to live once and enjoy many
All the lives
All the lives
All the lives
We weren't supposed to make it past 25
Now I'm here trying to find meaning
In a meaningless existence
But sad
I am far from
I just wish I knew more
I wish I could make it better for everyone
I hate to see things off balance
Some days I want to take on the world
Some days I'm kind of over it
But since this is my only known shot
I want to enjoy a lot
It's the libra in me
I always want everything
And nothing at the same time
Balancing beams take time

-Mr.West

www.ingramcontent.com/pod-product-compliance
Lightning Source LLC
Chambersburg PA
CBHW020715180526
45163CB00008B/3097